Amanda Theodocia Jones

A Prairie Idyl

And Other Poems

Amanda Theodocia Jones

A Prairie Idyl
And Other Poems

ISBN/EAN: 9783744677646

Printed in Europe, USA, Canada, Australia, Japan

Cover: Foto ©Thomas Meinert / pixelio.de

More available books at **www.hansebooks.com**

A PRAIRIE IDYL

AND OTHER POEMS.

BY

AMANDA T. JONES.

CHICAGO:
JANSEN, McCLURG, & COMPANY.
1882.

A Prairie Idyl

And Other Poems.

TO

MISS JANE W. KENDALL,

PROVIDENCE, R. I.

WHAT GIFT, MY FRIEND, CAN BE WORTHY OF YOU, TO
WHOM I OWE SO MUCH? BUT TAKE THIS LITTLE BOOK FOR
YOURS, AND KNOW THAT IF, OUT OF ALL THE WORLD, YOU
ONLY SHOULD LOVE THE VERSE, I SHOULD STILL REJOICE
TO HAVE WRITTEN IT FOR YOUR DEAR SAKE.

THE AUTHOR.

CONTENTS.

	PAGE
A PRAIRIE IDYL	9
SERVICE AND SACRIFICE	32
FATHER	36
HEART OF SORROWS	42
WHEN I CALL	53
THESE THREE	55
MERLIN	58
MARRIED	67
FAST ASLEEP	72
FROM SAURIAN TO SERAPH	76
WE TWAIN	91
A MORNING MADRIGAL	94
CROQUET	99
FREDDIE	102
DAWN	106

8   *CONTENTS.*

ROSES 108

LOVE'S LARGESS 114

ONE NIGHT 116

MOTHER 124

ONE OF THE TWELVE 133

SONNETS 149

A PRAIRIE IDYL.

I.

FOUR groves stood up in Western lands,
  Burr-oaks and poplars—thickets dense:
Four ways they faced, and linked their hands,
  From rude unreverent eyes to fence
    A closure fair and ample;
To well seclude the swaying wheat,
  The low luxuriant belt untilled,
From lawless tread of vagrant feet,
  From bursting wind-storms, frantic-willed,
    From brutes that rend and trample.

II.

That liberal field the granaries filled:
  But in the centre, screened and cool,

Deep-cradled, all its babbling stilled,
　　Peered out a limpid, lazy pool,
　　　　A-swoon with lulls and hushes;
Thence either way for many a rod,
　　From willows gray to brambles green,
Drove never plough-share through the sod,'
　　Flashed never scythe or sickle keen
　　　　Athwart the pipes and rushes.

III.

I would that place you might have seen:
　　Day after day, four seasons round,
I wandered there in shade or sheen,
　　And aye some pretty newness found--
　　　　Some trace of spirits tricksy.
There Nature had her willful way;
　　Toiled, lay at ease, frowned, sobbed, or smiled;
Was now a nimble sprite at play,
　　And now a queen, a laughing child,
　　　　A witch, a water-nixie.

IV.

Her winter-whiteness, undefiled,
　　Lent flowery grace to withered weeds,
Where hardy insects ran, and wild
　　　Brave snow-birds, searching after seeds
　　　　Through Boreal blore and bluster;
But when the drifts were April-kissed,
　　Marsh-marigolds on mound and fen
Through vapor soft (like nebulous mist,
　　All suns to astronomic ken),
　　　　Did gloriously cluster.

V.

And certain birds came seeking then
　　For nesting-nooks aloft or low:
Song-sparrow, blue-bird, robin, wren,
　　All new in love as one might know—
　　　　Deliriously trilling.
Ah, how the world enchanted them!
　　They fluttered, floated, flaunted by,

Set clinging feet on stalk or stem,
  And sent *roulades* into the sky
    As if it needed filling.

VI.

Sweet tunes, I know not how or why,
  Transfusing, enter sweetest flowers;
From where the songs went, far and high,
  Came down the violets in showers,—
    Blue, blue they were, and veiny;
With early crow-foot lamps ablaze,
  And avens-globes, that, rounding slow,
Are purple-dusk on thirsty days,
  But like betrothal rubies glow
    Rich red when all is rainy.

VII.

Waved everywhere those grasses low
  That bloom in yellow, blue, and white;
Green panicles tossed to and fro,

Out-floating sleaves and spinnings light—
  Sheer webs, diaphanous laces;
Dead gold of moneyworts outflung
  In royal largess, vetches rare,
Blue-flags with paling rainbows hung,
  Wood-sorrels exquisitely fair,
    Like wondering infant faces.

VIII.

Swept long processions here and there
  Of shooting-star flowers, rosy-stoled,—
Pink-purple crane's-bills, eyes a-stare
  At ragged neighbors overbold—
    Red-roots and Roman-candles.
No lack of scarlet bugs be sure,
  Of boat-flies, dragon-flies, and moths,
Sly lion-ants that trap and lure,
  With tiger-beetles fierce as Goths
    And terrible as Vandals;

IX.

Green span-worms, clambering like sloths,
   Cicadæ whetting horny beaks,
Gold spiders weaving silvery cloths,
   And bees that rob like very Greeks
      To feed their queen-commanders;
Red-mites that love the noon-day heats,
   Wood-nymphs and peacock butterflies,
Small aphides exuding sweets,
   Ichneumons dipped in Tyrian dyes,
      Like mimic Alexanders.

X.

Ah, then, all out of perfect skies
   Rushed in the lover-bobolinks!
Like Paganini, music-wise,
   Each bird will tell you all he thinks
      On just that one-stringed viol.
Should Handel, Mozart, Mendelssohn

Set awful challenges afloat,
This little master, all alone
   Half-way in Heaven, would tune his throat
   And dare them to the trial.

XI.

Even so: The sun is for the mote,
  And for the nautilus the sea;
Aërial space for one sweet note,
  The universe for you and me;
    God's own accords and closes
For *capel-meisters* great or small.
  O sealed stone lips of desert-sphinx,
Keep silence! . . . These will answer all. . . .
  Meantime my singing bobolinks
    Brought down the heavens in roses,

XII.

All single-wild, with hyssops, pinks,
  Miami-mists, pyrolas white,

Slight cleavers winding blossomed links,
　Fringed orchids, painted-cups fire-bright,
　　And delicate lobelias;
Blue skull-caps meant for reverend elves,
　Gay butterfly-weeds, their wings back-turned
From whirling flights to guard themselves,
　Wan arrowheads that poolward yearned
　　Like love-distraught Ophelias.

XIII.

But now the subtle sense discerned
　Attenuations faint and fine,
From where the sun at zenith burned
　Down to the shrinking water-line
　　That left the naiads dying;
Diminuendos organ-sweet,
　Charmed zephyrs vibrative and slow,
As, after bells have ceased to beat,
　The pleasured ear will hardly know
　　When hills forego replying.

XIV.

Began a crazy wind to blow;
  Loomed up a black and massy cloud;
Fell down the volumed floods that flow
  With volleying thunders near and loud,
    With lightnings broad and blinding.
A week of flying lights and darks,
  Then all was clear; from copse and corn
Flew grosbeaks, red-birds, whistling larks,
  And thrushes voiced like peris lorn,
    Themselves of Heaven reminding.

XV.

Deep trails my hasty hands had torn,
  Where, under fairy-tasselled rues,
Low vines their scarlet fruits had borne,
  That neither men nor gods refuse,—
    Delicious, spicy, sating.
As there through meadow red-tops sere
2

I toiled, my fragile friends to greet,
Out sang the birds: " Good cheer! good cheer! "—
" This way!"—" Pure, purity !"—" So sweet!"—
" See ! see! a-waiting—waiting! "

XVI.

I saw: Each way the rolling wheat,
  The wild-flower wilderness between,
Therein the sun-emblazoning sheet,
  Four ways the thickets darkly green,
    The vaporous drifts and dazzles;
Swift lace-wings flittering high and low,
  Sheen, gauzy scarves a-sag with dew,
Blown phloxes flaked like falling snow,
  ,Wide spiderworts in umbels blue,
    Wild bergamots and basils;

XVII.

And oh, the lilies! melted through
  With ocherous pigments of the sun!

Translucent flowers.of marvellous hue,
 Red, amber, orange, all in one,—
  Their brown-black anthers bursting
To scatter out their powdered gold:
 One half with upward looks attent,
As holy secrets might be told,
 One half with turbans earthward bent,
  For Eden's rivers thirsting.

XVIII.

And now the winds a-tiptoe went,
 As loth to trouble Summer-calms;
The air was dense with sifted scent,
 Dispersed from fervid mints and balms
  Whose pungent fumes betrayed them.
The brooks, on yielding sedges flung,
 Half-slept—babe-soft their pulses beat;
Wee humming-birds, green-burnished, swung
 Now here, now there, to find the sweet,
  As if a billow swayed them.

XIX.

Loud-whirring hawk-moths, large and fleet,
    Went honey-mad; the dipters small
Caught wings, they bathed in airy heat;
    I saw the mottled minnows all,—
        So had the pool diminished.
No Sybarite ever banqueted
    As those bird-rioters young and old:
The red-wing's story, while he fed,
    A thousand times he partly told,
        But never fairly finished.

XX.

Some catch the reeling oriole trolled,
    Broke off his black and gold to trim;
Quarrelled the blue-jay fiery-bold,—
    Or feast or fight all one to him,
        True knight at drink or duel;
New wine of berries black and red
    The noisy cat-bird sipped and sipped;

The king-bird bragged of battles dread,
　　How he the stealthy hawk had whipped—
　　　　That armed marauder cruel.

XXI.

While so they sallied, darted, dipped,
　　Slow feathered seeds began to sail;
Gray milk-weed pods their flosses slipped,—
　　More blithely blew the buoying gale,
　　　　And sent them whitely flying.
Rose up new creatures every hour
　　From brittle-walled chrysalides;
The yellow wings on every flower
　　With ringèd wasps and bumble-bees
　　　　Shone, Danae's gold outvying.

XXII.

Somewhat I missed of rhythmic ease,—
　　Warm equipoise of North and South:
Those silver weights of tropic seas

Bore down the scale; the days of drouth
  Caught gusts from vast expanses.
Now this way, that way, through the field
  The rattling reapers reaped the grain;
And much men talked of heavy yield,
  Who reckoned up their garnered gain
    And schemed for market-chances.

XXIII.

But I went out and faced the rain:
  I started up the prairie-hens,
Heard dripping mourning-doves complain,
  Amid the stubble saw the dens
    Of gophers, moles, and rabbits;
The quails and phœbe-birds and I
  A-wet were not afraid to roam;
Chipmunks and chittering squirrels shy
  From gleaning raids I followed home,
    Despite their wary habits:

XXIV.

Striped burrowers in the rooty loam,
    Tree-nesters, vaulters black and gray,
Was ever airling, brownie, gnome
    Or elf more deftly housed than they—
        Those rapid disappearers?
But now that arias all were sung
    And voices tired of wild *rolées*,
Sweet-sounding gitterns half-unstrung,
    One well might look for rare boquets
        Flung out from heavenly hearers.

XXV.

Almost one saw through yellow haze
    The laughing loiterers peering down:
With haste I crossed the fieldy ways,
    Nor stopped for briers nor held my gown
        From burrs and clinging loments.
Those milk-froth corymbs well I knew,
    Whose little dead-white clocks among

The gilded wheat had two moons through
　　Their triple-seeded pendules swung
　　　　To tell the lagging moments.

XXVI.

Now all abroad—though curtains clung
　　About the doors of noondays warm,
And dawns were chill—their circlets hung,
　　Self-fashioned in a flowery storm,
　　　　As when a snow-cloud settles.
And visible, yet pale the while
　　As cherubs seen through waning flame,
Those May wood-sorrels, infantile,
　　Bore once again their earthly name,
　　　　And dwelt among the nettles.

. XXVII.

All sunny-quick as quivering flame,
　　The ruby-throats hummed round about
Those nectarous thistles people blame,

And tipped their flasked elixirs out,
    Nor wronged one growing germen.
Soft-mirrored in the crimsoned pool,
    Plumed iron-weeds—Quixotes grim—
Kept witless guard. From lurkings cool
    Green pepperworts, that love to swim,
        Came floating up like mermen.

XXVIII.

Cone-flowers, corollas rim to rim,—
    Czarinas, queens, sultanas all,—
Stood crowned with beauty, stately-slim,
    By right divine the purple pall
        Magnificently wearing.
And radiant namesakes of the sun,
    From East to West a glittering band,
Bright-belted satellites every one,
    Turned on their axes, golden-grand,
        Celestial ardor sharing.

XXIX.

Along the turf-made bridge that spanned
    The narrow slough and sunken swale,
To keep the feet on firmer land,
    I, lingering, watched the ant-folk frail
        Prepare for bitter weather; .
Race in, race out, bear weighty spoils,
    Dig drains their humid hills to sluice,
Build cities, plan Herculean toils.
    Make war on giant-foes, grant truce,—
        Go jaunting off together.

XXX.

And now was every cleft of use,
    Some bronzed and sharded thing to hide,
Some brilliant creature, small and spruce,
    That late went rambling far and wide,
        The blue his sole pavilion.
Followed a blast, a rainy rush,

Careering clouds that met and crashed;
Then hints of frost,—a doubtful blush,
One sumach, like a palette, dashed
    With umber, gold, vermilion.

XXXI.

And out again the sunlight flashed;
An owl (his sleeping-time confused
With tempest-darkness), dazed, abashed,
    Fled forest-ward like one accused,
        Untimely flittings ruing:
Straightway those clannish sable-coats
    That clamor music steeple-high
(Sevenths, ninths, harsh inter-jarring notes),
    Wheeled out of ring, swooped down the sky,
        The blundering fowl pursuing.

XXXII.

"Aha! so you are caught!" said I:
    "Gray, tufted mouser—spoiler fell!

But who shall join the hue-and-cry
    To catch the felon crows as well?"
      With that, a rifle sounded;
And one whom pitying grace must reach
    If *he* escape, sprang out and laughed.
I went my way: what need of speech?
    The world was fair in spite of craft—
      Rose-apples yet abounded:

XXXIII.

Red, golden-cored, a stolen graft
    From Paradise; whose roots, green-girthed,
Such carmine spilth of suns had quaffed,
    One sacred seed, plucked out and earthed,
      Had vivified Sahara.
"But O, sweet-slumbering roses, sleep!"
    I sighed, "nor dream what weaklings shrink,
What plunderers prowl, what murderers creep,
    What souls, for dews of Hermon, drink
      The loathèd drops of Marah!"

XXXIV.

I saw the splendors southward sink,
   And turned to wonder while I might
At all those asters—azure, pink,
   Gray-blue, pure indigo, purple, white.—
      Not yet the cold had harmed them:
No blighting breeze, descending low,
   Had browned morasses greenly-deep,
Where shell-flowers orbed that never blow,
   But smile—forever sound asleep,
      As Viviane had charmed them.

XXXV.

Nor dared the frost his films to sweep
   Across the gentians fringed and blue—
Frail tabernacles veiled to keep
   Some holiest-holy place from view,
      Where never light should enter.
And now I called my slave of lamps,

To lift the field and move it thence,
With all its odors, fervors, damps,
Its blooms, its thickets hazel-dense,
The slopes from verge to centre;

XXXVI.

The storms blown in, one knew not whence,
The slumberous pool, the waterlings
The rose-lake dawns, the noons intense,
The glossy mites, the soaring things,
Tone-sweets and dissonances.
"Take up the place, O servant mine!"
I bade, "and bear it many a mile.
Since wizards trick, conjure, divine,
I too with woven spells would wile,
And practice necromancies.

XXXVII.

"May be," I said, and laughed the while,
"This fair King-Oberon's-Realm may seem

An Avalon, a flying isle,
  A soft-emblossomed poet's dream,
    A sun-and-wind suspension:
So let it swim in upper air,
  Made evident to mortal sight,—
A clear mirage, a rainbow-snare,
  A dewy exhalation slight,
    A spirit-like ascension.

XXXVIII.

" And if it waste in airy light,
  And if it melt and all diffuse,
And if it rise and vanish quite,
  Desired on high,—its lovely hues
    A white-translated seven,—
There are who gazing long will muse
  On world-similitudes serene,
Will smiling seize the beamy clues,
  Climb up from where GOD's earth is green,
    Look in, and see His Heaven."

SERVICE AND SACRIFICE.

I.

Whiter than dew-bleached flax or fleeces shorn,
Large-moulded as for treading out the corn,
Adorned with garlands looped from horn to horn,

Meek-faced and gentle—creatures without flaw,
Yoked in with banded gold and set to draw
From camp to camp the tables of the law,—

O happy oxen! thus approved to wear
Before the holy ark the symbols fair;
Light yokes of service for the LORD to bear!

II.

Struck down beside the altar—wonder-eyed,
The warm blood pouring from their gashes wide,
So wetting cleanly hoof and snowy hide,

With deep heart-pantings and with horns down-
    tossed
Among the wild-voiced people, desert-lost,
Paying of all their sins the crimson cost,—

O happy, happy oxen! thus to lie
And wait the swift flame circling down the sky,
Wrapped in the mantle of the LORD to die!

III.

But Aaron's priestly heart with pity yearned;
And when along the well-seared flesh out-burned
The fragrant oil, and tent-ward all had turned,

He drew the fine-twined hangings close around
The sacred court, and falling to the ground
Cried "Hear me, Lord, and let Thy grace abound!

"Thou, brooding still above the mercy-seat,
Are these red hands yet holy, and these feet
Painted with slaughter—is their service sweet?
   3

IV.

" And hear me yet (for I am faint with dread):
Before Thy graven word, with down-bent head,
Through sun and storm the beasts were wont to
    tread,

" While sweat of toil ran down like dropping rain:
Hadst Thou no sorrow, therefore, for their pain,
When all their life-blood washed the trampled
    plain?

" Are they who serve Thee chosen still to feel
About their throats the gashing of the steel,—
And Thou all wrath?   Herein Thyself reveal."

V.

Then Aaron lay and trembled; for the grace
And glory of the LORD had filled the place
MOST HOLY, so that none might show his face.

Out of the cloud a voice: " Have I not said,

' At morn and eve Mine altars shall be red?'
My people—are they not with bullocks fed?

" But know that I am GOD: Hath any need?
His toil and grief are Mine; with him I bleed:
Yoked in with Death that thou and thine may
    feed.

" Behold, who yields his life—an offering meet—
Thenceforth is yoked with LOVE! Arise and eat;
Thy hands are holy and their service sweet."

FATHER.

I.

I PLUCKED the bird-foot violets,
    Long-lobed, white-hearted, azure-pale,
      And odorous as heliotropes.
I said: "The sun in Heaven begets
    No fairer flower to scent the gale
      That fans the angel-haunted slopes:
I would beneath his eyes they grew
Who loved me when my years were few."

II.

Oh, he was gentle, generous, true!
    He loved his home, he loved his church,
      He pitied sinners everywhere;
The virtues of his friends he knew,
    But was not used their faults to search,

Nor found them—if they were not there.
Whoever else is sick or sad,
I have no doubt his life is glad.

III.

Ah me! if but the flowers he had!
  That leaning down from where he sings
    (Up-floated from the Heavenly plains
With that ineffable glory clad),
  He might behold the pallid things
    All newly washed in silver rains,
And pleased, reminded, murmur low:
"The earth bore violets long ago;

IV.

" My little daughter watched them grow:
  She travelled all the fields and dales,
    Crept under zig-zag fences rude,
Waded through shallow waters slow,
  Went shoulder-deep in meadow-swales,

And, charmed with woodland solitude,
Sank down at last, where, weighed with dew,
The pretty, pretty blossoms grew.

V.

"But these are holier of hue,
　Are lovelier far, more sweet of breath,
　　More altogether of the skies.
And can it be that world I knew
　Is reeling out from darks of Death?
　　And would my children all arise
And welcome me, if I should bend
My flight their way and so descend,—

VI.

"Hand holding hand as friend with friend?"
　And I believe that he would yield
　　His crown, and in the guise that hid
His soul before the journey's end,
　Would in the doorway stand revealed;

Would catch my hands as once he did;
Would lift me, kiss me, hold me high,
And bid me gaze into the sky.

VII.

Then I should see the stars go by;
  And I should see—nor die to see—
    Far-off, far-off, and very faint,
As through a glass, not eye to eye,
  Those who were bond but now are free,
    The well-beloved of that blest saint:
The two fair babes whose haste to go
Half-broke his heart, he loved them so;

VIII.

The pure young lad who yearned to know
  Some far, imagined, perfect land,
    Some rose-illumined Sharon's vale,
And hasted on through wind and snow
  With leaping foot and reaching hand

As Galahad to find the Grail,—
Till passed some burning charioteer
And snatched him; white with holy fear;

IX.

And that proud patriot-boy, all dear
  To God and us: no tongue can tell
    How deep the hurt when he went down;
And, over all, those gray eyes, clear
  As some unfathomable well
    Wherein all doubts and sorrows drown—
The mother, sighing: "Long I wait;
These are but four, and those are eight."

X.

Then I should see the light abate;
  Should lose and lose the vision fair;
    Should sink and sink, more closely pressed,—
Upon my lids a flowery weight,
  A scent of violets in the air;

Till he would lift me from his breast
All swooning—love me, lay me down,
Pass out, and so resume his crown.

HEART OF SORROWS.

I.

HER path breaks off,—she strikes some jutting
    wall
Night-hidden, thrust across. Thereby a rock
Light-shaken rolls: the tumult of its fall,
    The long, long silence and the far-down shock
        Take all her breath;
" For certain I have found" (so in her heart she
    saith)
        " The very haunts of Death."

II.

The mountain-air that should be blithe and loud
    Blown dense with dripping vapor doth not stir;
She feels it cling as though it were a shroud:

From Earth and Hell and Heaven it covers her.
If, fain to guide,
Some torch-upholding seraph tread the spaces
wide,
Yet will these shades abide.

III.

Howbeit she, groping, finds a stony bed—
Not strown upon with cones of cedar sweet,
But ragged, sharp to hurt: there rests her head
And will not shrink nor gather up her feet.
" If this may be,
And Death through these abysmal gates reach
after me,
All may be well" (saith she).

IV.

So waits on sleep: But still some tempest-thought,
Flame-winged, sweeps back that billow's soft
advance.

" And is this net-work of the flesh for naught"

    (She sighs) " but to be torn at every chance?

       Or doth it keep

Some desert-creature, ready for the outward leap,

      The rush, the tireless sweep?

V.

"O soul (and if there be a soul), unmeet

    For pastures green and rivers of delight!

   For thou wert cavern-born and fierce and fleet;

    A thing unclean, a prowler of the night.

      Lo, fettered fast,

What power, moved by thy moans, will set thee

    free at last,

      To rove Saharas vast?

VI.

" No doubt the Solitudes befit thee well:

    But how if One all shining cross the sands,

   With tranquil eyes that evermore compel,

And strange converting touch of holy hands;
In still accord
(Upbraiding not), full gently leading thee toward
The gardens of the Lord—

VII.

" Deep-set among the fair eternal hills,
With entrances of balsam-yielding fir
And date-sustaining palm; where (since He wills)
Thou shalt perceive far-off the murmurous stir,
The vestments white,
Of those melodious ones,—and, shadowed safe
from sight,
Shalt dream thy dreams of light?

VIII.

"Musing, how wondrous are the heights of fire!
What cool and fruitful vales their spurs secrete!
Awaiting through hushed æons of desire
Till thou shalt hear His voice, so loud, so sweet

With words that rule:

' Arise and enter in, thou who art white as wool,
    And let thy joy be full! '

IX.

"And oh, the many streams from Lebanon!
    The pleasant winds that flow out east and west,
From myrrh and frankincense and cinnamon!
    And oh, the beds of spice whereon to rest!
        And oh, the KING!
Lilies and clustering flowers and vines behold him
        bring,
        About thy feet to cling.

X.

" Ah me! the anguish, the devouring haste
    Of this, my soul, to touch the hands that save!
But if there be no gardens—if the Waste
    Stretch boundless on from empty grave to grave,
        If shriek and curse

And wail of furthest voices through the universe
    An infinite Woe rehearse,—

XI.

"Thou soul who rendest so the fleshly net,—
    Set free and to the desert-sweeps out-cast,
With all thy noon-tide thirst upon thee yet,—
    Shalt load, with desolate cries, the arid blast;
        Or crouch and wait
Beside the bitter springs whose waters will not
    sate
        Thine everlasting hate.

XII.

"But oh, to be so mocked! where late I lay,
    Choked by that cruel Ganges thick with mire
Men call Love's river, eyelids stiff with clay,
    Flung out to perish, scorched in winds of fire,
        Till One passed by,
And drew me from the flood and whispered 'It is I!
    Behold, thou shalt not die!'

XIII.

"How did my heart within me melt and yearn!
    What copious tears washed out my blinded
        eyes!
    Far up the silver steeps I saw Him turn,
        Then vanish—gathered to the awful skies:
            And without rest
I followed but to kiss some rock His feet had prest,
        And be forever blest.

XIV.

"The jostling crowds did jeer and buffet me
    Along the burning plains: At fall of night
    Among the steep-set rocks I shook to see
        Their olden beds uptorn by torrents white,
            The sheer descent
Beside whose soundless deeps I trod, fear-faint
        and spent,
            Nor found the way He went."

XV.

Here lifting up her voice she cries aloud:
  "Sore-beaten by the dread four winds that blow
From crag to crag the fell red-bosomed cloud,
  Oh, yet I thought to climb and near Him so!
    If still afar,
Only to wait and worship, silent as a star,
    Where all the glaciers arc.''

XVI.

Upstarting from her bed—as one who hears
  Supernal sighings and remote farewells,
With crash of final bolts that lock the spheres—
  " O Thou Serene '' (she mourns) " whose love
    excels!
    I may not reach
To clasp Thy robe and weep, and of Thy lips be-
    seech
    Their honey-dropping speech;—

4

XVII.

"Engirt with deathful snares: Yet hadst Thou
  seen
  Before the gulfs yawned black from north to
  south,
How had Thy tears of pity washed me clean!
How had I felt the kisses of Thy mouth!
  Now without doubt
The very gates of Hell, across the skies flung out,
  Have compassed me about."

XVIII.

Even at the word, from ledge to crevice steals
  An undulant motion, as of opening graves,
Or influent surges when the sea unseals
  The strong sepulchral door of ancient caves;
  Till, waxing bold,
Earth sends her thunders out: beneath the moun-
  tain rolled,
  They cleave its bases old.

XIX.

With stroke on stroke all down the wavering
  steep
  They cast this grieving one. . . . . But
    now a light
Smites darkness out from cope to centre deep:
  Hurled through the white abyss in headlong
    flight,
    From mortal harms,
The Angel of the Torch, whom Death nor Hell
  alarms,
    Upbears her in his arms.

XX.

She lies upon his breast like drifted snow:
  "My LORD and thine hath sent for thee " (he
    saith);
She feels the winds of Paradise outblow—
  Full fain is she to breathe their holy breath:
    Aloes and myrrh,

All the chief spices with their wafting wings astir,
Divinely comfort her.

XXI.

Such need hath soaring Love, the heavens make
way;
With all their stars they vanish as a scroll:
The King's pavilions, beautiful are they—
Behold, with sweets He satisfies her soul!
But I, less white,
Among the clefts of rocks, with creatures of the
night,
Hide me in sore affright.

WHEN I CALL.

I.

On the LORD when in sorrow I call
　And He pours out my drink,
From that cup of the wormwood and gall
　In rebellion I shrink:
　　All unworthy, unworthy,
Unworthy to drink of the gall.

II.

Over flowers while His gentle rain: fall,
　And their heads they lift up,
Still He gives me the wormwood and gall;
　Whispers, " Drink of the cup:
　　I would have thee be worthy,
Be worthy to drink of the gall."

III.

O my heart, cease for honey to call!
 Hush and heed the dear Voice:
" While I pour out the wormwood and gall,
 Be thou glad and rejoice;
  I have counted thee worthy,
Well worthy to drink of the gall."

IV.

Precious MASTER, whatever befall,
 Though I die at Thy feet,
Fill my cup with the wormwood and gall;
 It is sweet, it is sweet,
  Oh, how sweet to be worthy,
Made worthy to drink of the gall!

THESE THREE.

I.

I sAid of Love: "She hath no dwelling-place
  On earth or in the air:
Or near or far no man hath seen her face,
  That he should name it fair;
  The lion hath his lair
Among the olive-thickets cool and green,
The glittering serpent hath his balmy screen,
  And they who lightly bear
The weight of floods—those murderous creatures
   —sleep
Within the hushed recesses of the deep:
But as for Love, she is not here nor there."

II.

I said of Life: "Too well I know that queen
  Who bathes in blood her feet:

Hard by the soundless pit her gateways lean:
        Her hate is fiery-fleet;
        Her love is like the sleet
That pierces to the heart with bitter cold:
The timbers of her palace burn with gold,
        But she is all unsweet.
Haply she once was not, she shall not be;
Full to her throne-room creeps the crafty sea,
And secret waters weave her winding-sheet."

III.

I said of Death: " She is not young nor old:
        Her paths the heavens explore;
Times, times and countless times have made her
            bold:
        Yet enters she my door;
        Her lifted hands out-pour
Vials of odors—costly oil that drips
Upon the eyes till seals of soft eclipse
        Their olden sleep restore.

I have not seen her face, if she be fair;
If she be sweet I know not, I, nor care:
But what she is she will be evermore.

IV.

Death took me by the hands and kissed my lips:
    Thereafter I was still.
"Behold," she said, "One in the wine-press dips,
    That thou shouldst drink thy fill!"
    Did ever voice so thrill?
I turned to see if that were Death who spake;
Sun-like she smiled: "Thou who hast slept,
    awake;
    See thou my grapes distill
Their sweets from out the purple." Then I knew
Life's blood-bathed feet,—but named her Love,
    and drew
Within her banquet-house to feast at will.

MERLIN.

I.

I CRUSH wild grapes; I fill the cup
 With what the strong hand wins:
For when my vassal-star is up,
 My wizard-work begins.
  I tread the magic round;
  I shake the solid ground;
The hurricane, whose hollow wings
 Drag through the snow of both the poles,
Dies when I sign; the grewsome things
 That gibe and mock tormented souls
  Aye hush, and heed my word;
   Back to the clouds they leap,
   Their lurid ways are steep:
But till he hears who never heard,

Who roams and hath no rest,
And till the heart that never stirred
Rocks in his kingly breast,
My phantom sheaves I reap,
I delve in sorceries deep.

II.

Uprears the star: now will I quaff,
For blessing or for bane,
The drink that makes the white gods laugh,
The black gods howl with pain.
Though they be fain and loth,
Like sonship have they both;
Ripe math is theirs and vintage red;
The sacred sour-and-sweet they pour;
Deep in the dish dip hallowed bread;—
And these will sink, and those will soar.
O tangled bird and snake!
O world that joys and drees!
O glad and fell decrees!

Till he shall come his thirst to slake
Who never drank of wine,
And smile: "Brave Merlin, hearts must ache,
But health to thee and thine!"
I rob my nights of ease;
I wade through sable seas.

III.

All spells that ever mortal wrought
To daunt the demon-train,
All moonlight gossameres up-caught
Are webbed about my brain.
Nathless, when late I slept
One near me wept and wept:
"Oh, wear thy silver shoon to-night,
And see thou pluck no water-weed;
But say thy potent weird aright
Full thrice, for sore will be thy need.
Be thine enchantments wise;
For when the North out-slips

Her fiery-masted ships,
Then will he lean across the skies:—
O Merlin, guard thee well;
For thou shalt read, in midnight eyes,
What none may hear or tell:
The while thy wine he sips,
With dread, desiring lips."

IV.

And now I don my charmèd shoon;
I ponder thrice the text;
I trouble not the rathe round moon;
I leave the sea unvexed;
I nail the windy gates
Where wild Arcturus waits;
And ever, while the lissome flame
Runs round my trench of precious oil,
I kneel and write the HOLY NAME
In awful symbols on the soil.
Awake, O North! forego

Thy polar couches dim,

While yet thy star may swim

Unswallowed of the swathing snow.

Send out thy ships of fire,

And burn him hither, friend or foe;

For great is my desire

To clash loud brim with brim,

To rise and strive with him.

V.

Her smouldering coals have caught the gales,

Her masts are zenith-high:

How fair outswell the yellow saiis

Against a paling sky!

Those glassen floods are wide

Wherethrough her vessels ride:

They follow East, they follow West,

They follow South, for weal or woe;

Now first within his wieldy breast

The mighty heart swings to and fro.

All dark from battle-sods
   His samite raiment fine,—
   All brackish from the brine:
He feels that spur of scourging rods,
   He treads the gulfs of loss;
He knows that wanton thirst of gods;
   He leans the heavens across.
     I bruise my grapes for wine—
     Good health, sweet brother mine!

VI.

I know thee, that thy name is Death,
   Thou drainer of the blood:
Thy lips I gift with dainty breath;
   I crown thee, leaf and bud.
     Through near unlawful eyes
     I draw thy proud replies:
"Sweet health, O Merlin, gentle king,
   Forever wait on thine and thee!
But wilt thou quit thy ghostly ring?

And art thou brave to strive with me?"
Now never youth so burned
To stride his warling steed,
To slay the dragon-breed,
As I, the yet Unthrown, have yearned
To meet thee fair in fight;
And, till thy riddles I have learned,
To wrestle, mind and might:
Or thou or I must bleed,—
So sore is this my need!

VII.

Beyond my trench, whose failing oil
Upwafts the wasteful flame,
Unclothed of sorceries I toil,
.Yet breathe the HOLY NAME.
And art thou wroth to hear?
And dost thou quake with fear?
Art thou that hewer of the rocks,
That builder of the towers of Bel?

Hast thou the master-key that locks
  The clanging doors of Heaven and Hell?
    For rapture or for dole
      Thou liest, struck with steel,
     Thy heart beneath my heel!
Art thou that keeper of the scroll
  Whereon the lightnings write,—
That bids thee seize and chain the soul,
  Or whirl it, starred, from sight?
    Though thunders seven outpeal,
    I break the seven-fold seal.

VIII.

I read: "When Death has quenched his thirst
  Where Merlin strips the bine,
His trusty lance shall win, who first
  Has named the Name Divine.
    Suns' veins for him shall bleed;
    Bees' honey him shall feed:

5

Last, One, full strong to soar and sink,

   Heaven-veiled in purples vast and dim,

Will break his bread, will share his drink,

   Will rise and sweetly strive with him;

      Heart-pierced will strike him down,—

        Will whisper: ' Thou shalt know,

     Fair-son, my weal and woe ;

Shalt follow where the black gods frown,

   Self-soaked in bitter brine,

With me there plunge and deeply drown,

   Spill out thy blood as wine ;

      Uplift them friend or foe,—

      So kiss them white as snow ! ' "

MARRIED.

I.

I ENTERED Broadway where the rush is the
greatest,—
You must wait by St. Paul's ere you cross,
Near the grave stones green-fretted with moss;
Lips have mouldered long decades ago, at the
latest,
That Love used to kiss:
The dead were on that side, the living on this.

II.

Up the street arm-in-arm walked a man and a
woman:
Their garments were ancient and odd:
Centenarians under that sod

Might have fashioned and worn them, what time
they were human,
And dust was in bloom:
These two, they were old, they were ripe for the
tomb.

III.

Now I said to myself, as I wondered and watched
them:
"They are poor; their good clothes are worn
out;
They have ransacked the garret, no doubt,—
Mended garbs of ancestress and ancestor, botched
them,
But so done their best,
Caught in Poverty's grip, to be decently dressed."

IV.

While half the crowd turned to look after, or
tarried

To see them so queerly attired

(Yet the camlet had once been admired),

Some wag struck an attitude, crying: "Just mar-

- ried,—

And off on a tour!"

Then he laughed out aloud, like a jolly young

wooer.

V.

Ten steps, and I faced the twain, each to each

smiling:

Amused, as it seemed, with the jest,

And meekly content for the rest:

Dear Love in one moment their sorrows exiling

Down fifty years' life

To that glad hour when GOD said, "Be husband

and wife."

VI.

And if ever I saw how Love's glory embrightened

A countenance, wrinkles and tan,

This I saw in the smile of the man
As he looked on his bride, with her brown hair all
whitened,
Her beauty all dim,—
The one lovely face in the wide world for him.

VII.

Ah, but for his help how the worn feet had stum-
bled!
For the eyes were as blind as a stone
That had dwelt on one sweetheart alone,—
Her sorry old bridegroom, who saw her so hum-
bled,
And led her along
As a king leads his queen through the midst of
the throng.

VIII.

Just married!—eternity stretching before them;
Suns kindled to lure them from earth;

Full wine-jars for second-day mirth:
Revered be the vestments, the lovers who wore
them—
This queen and this king!
God's host will their epithalamium sing.

FAST ASLEEP.

I.

Oꜰ, to be buried, ever so deep,
  Under the myrtle tree!
Always and always fast asleep
  As the nereids are in the sea.
With the ghostly stories of earth all told,
Caught to the heart of the matron old,
Veiled in her lustrous green and gold
  As only the dead can be:
Pale and pulseless, mute and cold,
    Calm as the sisters three,
    Content with the dread decree,
    Nothing to do or dree.

II.

Oh, to be lost and lost and lost

To world and star and sun!
To river and forest, flame and frost,
  To battles wasted or won;
Lost to the throbbing of hearts elate,
To the horror of lives accursed of Fate,
To the soul I love and the face I hate,
  To the lips I seek or shun;
Stilled and lying in awful state,
    Shrouded away from the sun,
    With a shroud of the white fleece spun,—
    Forever and ever undone.

III.

Sweetly the nereids rest in the deep:
  Once they were singers proud;
None remember the eyes asleep,
  Or the sea-harps rich and loud.
But they sang till the dwellers of isle and town
Sank in the wild wave, fain to drown,
And they sang till the cruel mermen brown

Were a weeping, wondering crowd;
And they sang and they sang till the gods came
down
In fire to the singers proud,
And the sky to the sea was bowed,
And the sea was a crimson cloud.

IV.

Hither, come hither, marvellous Death,
Under the myrtle tree:
With lips that never have breathed a breath,
Drop honey of kisses free;
Till the last, last terrible story is told,
And I creep to the heart of the matron old,
Wrapped in her rustling green and gold,
Always and always free:
Grand and griefless, pure and cold,
As only the dead can be;
Wan as the sisters three,
Or the nerieds under the sea.

V.

Buried—and never a bell will toll,
  However the wind may sweep:
But always the world will roll and roll,
  And the tides around her creep.
And never a dweller of isle or town
Will mourn because of our lost renown,
And never a murmuring merman brown
  Will sorrow under the deep,
Nor sigh; no, not if the gods come down
    From the heights so far and steep,
    For a songless world to weep!
    And we shall be fast asleep.

FROM SAURIAN TO SERAPH.

I.

'T was a poor blacksmith did the work before;
  The pony interferes: you'll please get down;
I served apprenticeship seven years or more
  In London, ere Victoria wore the crown,
And I can shoe a horse with any man.
  [*Whoa there! stand still!*] . . . . I saw you
      on the road;
You ride as well as any lady can,—
  And he's a trim beast, worthy such a load.

II.

Fine day for riding: how the sun laughs out!
  Look at those rapids, glittering down the fall.
And have you heard the birds? they shout and
      shout—

Sun, birds, and waters—well, I love them all.
Yet once I was a brute: what was a bird,
   That I should stay to watch him in his flight?
Forty-two battles I've been in, and heard
   My horse's hoofs clang hard through every fight.

III.

Oh, then I had rich times! then I was proud!
   You should have seen: the sabre in my hand
Was just one red, and dripping like a cloud!
   There never was a life so glad and grand.
But when the last ball's ricochet made rout,
   And the last shell tore up the bloody sod,
I used to call my corps of blacksmiths out
   And drive the nails till every beast was shod.

IV.

"Rest?" Bless you! have such creatures need
      of rest?
   Look, girl! you've heard of that old Saurian age

When scaly monsters crowded breast to breast ·
　And tusk to tusk in one destroying rage?
I do believe that mad, blind, battling force
　That smote so at the bass of earth's great harp,
Through finer ages rolled its cloudy course,
　And shook my frame with thunder swift and
　　sharp.

V.

For there's a law that sums each cycle—gives
　Its full, stern impulse to the life beyond;
And every spirit, weak or strong, that lives
　Is nerved to feel such urgings and respond.
Oh, they refine, I grant, through starry fire!
　The Saurian rage that lights a seraph's eyes
Is just that still white flame that sends him
　　higher,
　With "Alleluia!" challenging the skies.

VI.

That for the seraph: but for me you know,

Why I was in the sloughs—a very brute!
In stifling airs my soul began to grow,
  Mire-clogged—as all GOD's grandeur to refute!
Yet more than Saurian in spite of all:
  I felt the winds blow cooler now and then;
Down the wide wastes heard far sweet voices call,
  And knew my beasts and dimly yearned for men.

VII.

I'll drop my metaphors: you'll understand·
  I served ten years because I loved to slay;
And having fought, was fed. Oh, it was grand!
  My brutish blood ran richer day by day.
I had a Quaker mother . . . . well, she died:
  I think till then she never lived—in me.
My father and myself fought side by side,
  Grim battle-mates: small chance for her, you see.

VIII.

But after death I saw her—where she came,
  A spirit pale, right through my furnace-heat:

"Such fire and no one warmed? O son, for
    shame!"
And I fell down and trembled at her feet.
That proved me man; for mark, no beast will wake
    At call of angels! I began to stir,
And question of the sloughs what way to take
    If I might rise and follow after her.

IX.

I left the service when my time was out,
    And crossed from Canada to settle down;
But I could only drift and drift about,
    And wander drearily from town to town.
One day it chanced I came upon a crowd
    Mobbing an orator—a boorish gang:
"Bring on your rotten eggs!" one called aloud;
    "We 'll hear no Abolitionist harangue."

X.

Well, I went in for sport: I filled my hat

And shot out straight (I never miss my aim);
It struck the man between the eyes,—at that
A laugh went roaring upward like a flame.
Just then a hand fell softly on my head:
"My man, has thee no better wares to vend?"
I turned (an egg half-raised): "Let be!" he said;
"Thee does n't know what thee is doing, friend."

XI.

Oh, how ashamed I was!—dyed red clear through!
I felt as small as any crawling worm.
Meantime a shower of stones above me flew:
"Yon fellow 'll flinch," I thought; but he stood
    firm.
Then like a lion startled with the hunt,
Whose sudden voice will strike the Arabs·mute,
All quivering wrath, I bounded to the front:
The very man in me unleashed the brute!

6

XII.

What happened further?   Nay, I hardly know!
  I meant just slaughter. "Touch him if you
    like!"
I roared: "Come on! I 'll give you blow for blow!
  Look! here 's a British fist! now feel it strike!"
I routed them—the cowards! made them fly
  Howling as if the world was like to end.
.And then I found my Quaker: "Well," said I;
  "I 've sold my wares!" He laughed: "Thee 's
    valiant, friend;

XIII.

"Thee 'd better keep with us; we 'll do thee good."
  And so they did: A truer life I found,
Caught at the golden lines of brotherhood
  And scrambled from the mire to safer ground.
You see those Quaker mothers took me in,
  And fed me, starving, with the holy bread

Christ brake among the twelve; and what can win
   Like those dear words the lowly Master said?

XIV.

And there I learned the story of the slave
   (That earthquake-tremor sure to rend the land);
And, signing me that I should haste to save,
   In every cloud I saw my mother's hand;
In every wind I heard her voice: "*My son:*
   And will thy boasted strength but serve to slay?
Under the cross of labor, scourged, undone,
   They need thee who have fallen by the way."

XV.

So many years I kept the secret track,
   To guide those straying negroes into rest;
And when their masters followed, sent them back
   The poorer by a slave or two at best.
But sometimes, when pursuit was fierce and hot,
   I caught some cruel fellow with a grip,

And bound him hand and foot: I kept my shot
  For bloodhounds—but I lent his slaves my whip.

XVI.

For I was brutal still: and yet I learned
  All Blackstone in those days, and much of Coke;
I read the histories where their battles burned,
    And laid me under Shakespeare's "gnarlèd
      oak,".
(Whose acorns sprout in every soil to make
  The round earth green!); loved Junius, Cicero,
And Whittier; made the sober Quakers quake
  For laughter, with my violin and bow.

XVII.

Meanwhile I took a wife;—for what's a man
  With all his loves at dry-rot in his heart?
Unseasoned timbers—bound to mar the plan
  And sink the ship, however fair the chart.
But a good wife is like a strong sweet breeze

That searches in and out and keeps all right:
Ah, yes! and fills the sails till childly seas
   Leap up and clap their hands in sheer delight!

XVIII.

There's nothing like a wife; and mine's a queen.
   When from his egg that huge war-python crept,
She let me go; and yet if you had seen
   How hard it was, I think you would have wept.
But I—my happy heart beat fast and loud
   (Made greater by Love's ichor in the veins),
To share—my horse and I—through fire and cloud
   That world-wide rapture of the hurricanes.

XIX.

I never blame the Rebels: but be sure
   I do not blame myself for shooting them.
There's not a wind in Heaven so cool and pure,
   It has not brushed some martyr's blazing hem!
There's not a waving flower throughout the skies

So white, it is not rooted deep in mud!
Between the suns there's not a seraph flies
That somehow, somewhere, did not wade in
blood!

XX.

Why, even you—bright-glancing—you, who stand
So lightly poised, like any forest-bird,
That if you did not urge me (voice and hand
And ardent eye), I should not speak a word
For fear you'd soar! There'll come a time you'll
set
Those milky teeth—will clasp your girdle well,
And on the nearest stone the knife you'll whet
To flay some scarlet dragon late from Hell!

XXI.

But, grander still, from out your gold you'll sift
That sand of self, the whole deep mountain
through:

Because of Love, such weights of care you'll lift,
  The sweat of blood will gather fast as dew.
God help you, girl!· for all the deaths you'll dare;
  Wind, frost and flood, serpent and beast you'll
    greet:
Till one shall come and hale you by the hair
  Straight to the fagots ! . . . . There's the secret
    sweet.

XXII.

I've guessed it partly.   Pausing in the fight
  One day, behold my mother standing near!
And all around her played such tongues of light
  As would have made the bravest martyr fear.
More pallid than the dead, and waving slow
  Her hands toward the South: "*I bore thee,
    child,*"
She said, "*with bitter pangs: but thou shalt
    know
  A larger grief than mine!* "—and then she
    smiled.

XXIII.

Now, when my soul from that dread trance awoke

(Low reeling in the saddle, reins all slack),

A man I loved came plunging through the smoke

With half a score of Rebels on his track.

I flung between; I galloped to and fro;

Broad sweeps of sabre barred the fell pursuit:

But so they took me prisoner; caged me so

All bleeding; starved me as a jungle brute.

XXIV.

Two summers . . . . "What of them?"   Hush!

never wish

To read those inky tablets of the flood;

Down by the altar set no silver dish

To catch the dripping of the bullock's blood;

Ask not of fires that drank all currents up,

Aye, emptied out the hollows of the sea!

Nor dare with those young lips to press the cup

They drain who travail in Gethsemane!

XXV.

They brought me home, an idiot, to my wife;
　My children kissed me, and I did not know.
Just one last drop was in the springs of life,
　And long they watched if any wave could flow.
It came at last—slow rising to the brim,
　The deep sweet fountain drawn through veins
　　of Death,
Out of that dear abundant Heart of Him
　Most Calm, who lives all life, who breathes all
　　breath.

XXVI.

And now I blow the coals, I pare the hoof
　(God labors; so must we); I come and go;
But when some lightning rends this rainy roof—
　An instant stroke (they say it will be so),—
Ah, then, all drenched and charred beneath,
　above
All supple grace!—who knows what holy cheei

Of kisses me will greet? what whorls of Love
　　Will fold me round, sphere rolled on rosy
　　　sphere?

XXVII.

This certain: That dread Power, so prone to
　　waste,
　　That bids the Saurian gnash devouring teeth,
The gunner plant his guns, the martyr haste
　　To perish in the fagots' flaming sheath,
Nerves still some white and virile hand that flings
　　Wide open all the gateways of the sky;
Rounds out some seraph's. voice, the while he
　　sings
　　His "Holy, holy is the LORD MOST HIGH!"

WE TWAIN.

I.

Oh, Earth and Heaven are far apart!
But what if they were one,
And neither you nor I, Sweetheart,
Had anyway misdone?
When we like singing rivers fleet
That cannot choose but flow,
Among the flowers should meet and greet,
Should meet and mingle so,
Sweetheart,
That would be sweet, I know.

II.

No need to swerve and drift apart,
Or any bliss resign:

Then I should all be yours, Sweetheart,
　　And you would all be mine.

But ah, to rush, defiled and brown,
　　From thaw of smirchèd snow,
To spoil the corn, beat down and drown
　　The rath red lilies low, —
　　　　Sweetheart,
　I do not want you so!

III.

For you and I are far apart,
　　And never may we meet,
Till you are glad and grand, Sweetheart,
　　Till I am fair and sweet;
Till morning-light has kissed us white
　　As highest Alpine snow,
Till both are brave and bright of sight,
　　Go wander high or low,
　　　　Sweetheart;
　For GOD will have it so.

IV.

Oh, Heaven and Earth are far apart!
 If you are bond or free,
And if you climb or crawl, Sweetheart,
 Can no way hinder me.
But see you come in lordly state,
 With mountain winds aglow,
When I by dazzling gate shall wait
 To meet and love you so,
   Sweetheart,—
That will be Heaven, I know.

A MORNING MADRIGAL.

I.

My cottage-roof with flickering green is draped,
　Whose sun-drawn tides, in haste to reach the
　　　light,
Have burst their viny channels, whence escaped
　They roll their gold and scarlet into sight.
　　O foliage, rich with bloom,
Sail in on fragrant airs, and grace my curtained
　　　room!

II.

How tenderly they live—these underlings!
　Lo, on the new-rosed brier, an oriole guest,
　Wing-weary, flutters down and sings and sings
　As if all Heaven were in his little breast.
　　Ah, sweet and very sweet!
Trill on, delicious voice,—the silence still defeat.

III.

But he is dead—my love, who made the earth
    Yield me all rosy marvels of the year;
Who fed with laughter sweet life's morning-
        mirth;
    Who filled my cup with dripping honeys clear,
    Who made all pleasures mine,—
The hearth, the green-roofed hall, and Love's white
        lamp to shine.

IV.

He lies upon the trestles, calm as Fate:
    But not the less burn red, thou clinging vine;
His lips move not—their music died of late:
    Yet keep the brier, thou bird, astir with thine;
    Be glad, O world, and fair!
So may this loving soul awhile his flight forbear.

V.

Cast by the trailing sheet that hides the dead,

Low sleeps my boy, who bears his honored
name;
The yellow ringlets blown about his head,
His cheeks a scarlet miracle of flame;
The fallen hands at rest
In drifts of blossoms culled to deck the shrouded
breast.

VI.

Forgotten purpose: Yet how sweet they are!
Such flowers as children love—the creamy
phlox,
Fiery nasturtion-blooms that flash afar,
And candytufts and ruby hollyhocks,
And great carnations red
As if their veins ran rich with blood of Summers
dead.

VII.

His tears are spent—my darling! let him sleep:
Soft be his dreaming as the breath of flowers.

Across his curls a shadowy hand will creep,
Athrob with purer, finer life than ours.
O earth, your joys arraign!
With light and luminous threads this passing soul
detain.

VIII.

For oh, to feel him gone!—some upward way,
Strown white with lilies for his wandering feet;
Heaven's rippling rivers dashed in snowy spray,
And every flying breeze with treble sweet:
So fair, so far and fair,
Remembrance well might sink and slumber una-
ware.

IX.

Ah, wrong him not, poor heart! since Love
alone,
Whose thoughts are all familiar with the sun,
Can face with tranquil eyes that Summer-zone
Where sunk in flowers the living waters run.

He draws me while he soars;

My soul, half-sainted, floats and nears seraphic
shores.

X.

Be strong, my soul, for Love is ever strong;

Draw him and all his life of beauteous days:

Thy wistful sighs shall thrill his world of song,

Thy smiles shall light its lily-whitened ways.

Behold, all hours we share;

He conscious of the earth, and I of Heaven aware!

CROQUET.

I.

Gate carved in granite, with griffins at rest,
Arches built grandly to welcome the guest,
Elm-guarded avenue, dim as sea-caves,
Sweep of quaint bridges and rush of clear waves,
Group of acacias, dark cluster of pines,
Mansion half-whelmed in a torrent of vines,
Fountain a shower of fire, lake a soft gloom,
Garden unrolling broad ribbons of bloom,
Lawn smooth as satin and air cool as spray,—
Roland and Christabel deep in croquet!

II.

Christabel—Roland, the flower of our clan,
Noble and bountiful,—match them who can.

He fleet and supple, yet strong as young Saul;
She in ten thousand the fairest of all;
He quick to anger, but loving and leal;
She true and tender, though tempered like steel;
Both of all weathers, fine dew and fierce hail,
Ice on the mountain and flowers in the vale:
All their still frostiness melted away,
Just for that nonsense—a game of croquet!

III.

Only croquet?   Never trust to the game,
Kindling such raillery, feeding such flame;
Keeping such bird-bolts of laughter in flight,
Tossing such roses of battle in sight!
Roland in triumph and ready to scoff,
Christabel poising her mallet far-off,
Ball speeding on with the wind in its wake,
Smiting its rival and hitting the stake!
Who is the victor?   Proud Roland, at bay,
Captures the hand that has won at croquet.

IV.

Now is their magic enchainment complete;
Haughty, shy Christabel—far-away sweet,
Caught in that wind from the Aidenn of souls,
Blushes rose-bright as red snow of the poles!
Out of all lovers match these if you can;—
Spotless, great-hearted, the flower of our clan.
If they should quarrel—half-right and half-
    wrong—
Oaks root them deeper when breezes are strong.
Now may Love lead them away and away,
Through the wide Heavens, from that game of
    croquet!

FREDDIE.

I.

PRECIOUS FREDDIE, just breathing his last,
Gave one and another his wee hand to kiss;
  Looked long at mamma, and so lovingly passed,
    Fearing height nor abyss.

II.

But what of the babe after this?
Did the small-featured cherubim haste and make
      room?
Did any uphold him, lest aught he should miss
Of the blaze and the bloom,—

III.

Dust rendered to dust in the tomb?

Oh, sweet, through GOD's silence, to ponder and
dream .

With what gradual glory, through vanishing
gloom,

His good-morrow might gleam!

IV.

Not thro' sepulchre door-ways would stream,
In one burst, all that excellence.   Rather, I think,

Little Freddie would wake at some wandering
beam

Darting in past the chink:

V.

While down on his breast there would sink
Some rich-tinted flower, and he, drowsy, would

peer

Through the shadows, each way, to see who
dropped the pink;

Reach out hands, have no fear,—

VI.

And the Presence would smile and draw near.
So lifted, caressed, he would nestle and cling,
Drop lids, fall on slumber as babes do who hear
The hushed mother-voice sing.

VII.

Now indeed would the grave-doors out-swing,
And the.dawn break: but Freddie, asleep, would
not know,
Till some soft hand magnetic would wave, as a
wing,
To and fro, to and fro,

VIII.

Over infantine limbs, and the flow
Of new life-tides, like quicksilver streams, would
rush through,
Charged with vigor angelic; the wan face would
grow
Like June-roses in hue,—

. IX.

Blush-lovely, yet cool as the dew.
Then the child would leap up, brave to traverse
the spheres—
Bright or dark, so they led to the dear ones he
knew,
Sitting blinded with tears!

X.

When we wake at the end of our years,
In the half-open tomb, dropping pinks, will he
stand?
Heart-thrilled with babe-laughter, forgetting
our fears,
Shall we kiss his wee hand?

DAWN.

I.

Too LONG has been the night; my veins are chill;
　Unhappy, scaring dreams have wasted sleep.
For buried Memory would have her will,
　Cross grave-yard bounds, wring ghostly hands
　　　and weep
About the keeping-places of Desire,
　Lamenting murdered Love; winds without rest
Would shrill thro' ruined rooms, where never fire
　Upon the hearth flames up for heir or guest.

II.

I will arise, go forth and meet the sun:
　Astarte whitens heaven, and, where the sea
Steals round the world, pellucid ripples run:
　I will arise, fling open doors—go free.
Already shoots the gold athwart the sky,
　Already breaks the scarlet through the foam;

Lo, lightly loosed, the wavering shadows fly,
    Flits out the darkness from the desolate home!
And we are glad, are glad, my heart and I,
    And we are glad, are glad, and fain to roam,—
To quit the ivied, haunted, skeleton-place,
    The spidery mansion, rafterless and lone;
To flee that ancient woe of pictured face,
    These hollow-sighing halls where spectres moan.

III.

Already chirpers cry and warblers sing,
    Already lilies weep and roses blush:
Higher and higher, through the skies a-swing,
    Shines the sun-pendulum. I leap, I rush
Out from the chambers, down the swerving stair!
    My heart and I escape the falling towers.
Already wings of eagles beat the air;
    I run, I laugh, I bury feet in flowers.
O welcome, welcome, welcome infinite Light!
It is the dawn: too long has been the night.

ROSES.

I.

In that garden of yours by the sea
You have willed shall be mine when we wed
(So kingly your gracious decree!)
 There are " roses on roses," you said;
I can fancy their opulent grace,
Where they glimmer—each one in her place:
 Mystic roses . . . . These lavish of red
 (One would say their hearts bled);
 Those deeper—a skyful of light
 Would not alter their night;
 Here yellow—gold-leaf newly shred ·
 (Egypt mourning her dead);
 There white—calyx-coffined, struck through
 With that grief of the dew:

Ah, sweet, deathly sweet they must be,
In that garden of yours by the sea!

II.

But wait—I have somewhat to say:
　Forgive while the bitter winds blow;
I have heard of your roses to-day,—
　Who gathered them Summers ago:
Who, fain in your Heaven to dwell,
Was caught in the flames of your Hell;
　　Wrapped around, all her raiment of snow
　　Strown in ashes below;
　　Drenched with tears and left ghastly and
　　　stark,
　　Just to die in the dark!
I have heard,—for a fountain, you know,
　Once opened, will flow,
Till, however far off, you may fill
　The white cup, if you will.

I have drunk those salt waters astray:
You will wait—I have somewhat to say.

III.

First: spare me your evil-wrought shield—
   Gules on azure! . . . . I know the device
When a knight like yourself takes the field,
   And the trumpets bray out in a trice;
When heralds and pursuivants meet,
Through a babble of voices too sweet:
    "Look! his armor was bought with a price!
     Be not over-nice:"—
    Though down in your donjon so deep,
     Awake or asleep,
    Lies that dragon whom nought will suffice,
     And they see you entice
    Fair maidens to thrust in at need
     (For a dragon must feed!) . . . .
Nay, close your barred visor, sit steeled;
But down with your blood-blotted shield!

IV.

I, a woman, will hurl out my lance,
  Though a worldful of hisses should greet.
Did I love you this morning, perchance?
  Did I blush when your kisses were sweet?
Oh, we of the roses will glow
  In all lights—from above or below;
    And ever Hell's lava-tides beat
      Close under our feet!
    But you of the fires never quail
      Though we shrivel and fail,
    When your wiverns and griffins we meet
      In their cursèd red heat!
    To your donjon, O Knight of renown,
      Shall I follow you down?
All that dragonish craving enhance?
As for me, I will hurl out my lance.

V.

For what is this miracle-rose

Of womanhood holy and white,
But the marvel of GOD, where he glows
In the bush, and we kneel at the sight!
Where His spirit, unsearchable, breathes
Creative, through luminous sheathes,
Till souls are revealed out of night
In such glory of light,
HIS prophet would put off the shoe! . . .
But prophets like you
Snatch all cressets to quicken the flight
Of that Pagan fire-fright,
When your victims lie, strangled and pale,
On the alters of Baal.
See Egypt's brute-god where he lows!
Shall he trample earth's miracle-rose?

VI.

All is said: You will pass from my door.
What? you cry that you love me, and cling?
All ashamed of that armor you wore,

At my feet casque and corslet you fling?
Rise: Here is a ROSE for your shield:
Ride away to your donjon, new-steeled;
  Unchain that fell beast,—loose the wing,
    Bid the drawbridge out-swing;
  Full fair in the face of the sun
    Be your fierce battle won;
  Strike his heart till its currents you bring
    Spouting hot from their spring;
  Wash away your attainture of shame
    In that river of flame:
So come to me, dipped in bright gore!
I will love you. . . . . Pass out from my door.
  8

LOVE'S LARGESS.

I.

SAY not you love me: spare to speak with guile:
Too well your faltering speech and failing smile
 Betray Love's secret want. "This shel-
  tered niche,"
 (Sighs the lone soul), "this haunt with ver-
  dure rich,
Is all so sweet I needs must rest awhile,
And from these silver-heavy mosses wile
 Their slow, cool drops: because my thirst is
  great,
 Content to curve the hand and woo and wait.
But oh, to find some ruddy-templed isle,
Palm-rooted in the lotos-laving Nile!

And oh, to leap and plunge in that divine white
    rush
From Afric's golden peaks, with fiery clouds a-
    flush!"

II.

Nay, springs lie deep, and hearts are not so small.
Behold if any love me, he shall call—
  Osiris unto Isis through the dawn
  "Arise! my world awaits,—its veil withdrawn,
Its ghastly coverts bared from wall to wall,
Its deserts unredeemed, its gods in thrall.
  Be certain there are monsters in the seas,
  And eagles on the crags; but fear not these,
Nor let the wild loud-laughing storms appall:
For I am with you—I, who rule them all."
Then shall I hear and answer, breaking from the
    gloom,
"I come with all sweet waves: make broad your
    paths for bloom!"

ONE NIGHT.

I.

As ONE whose indolent hand forgets to hold
 A falling flower, I loosed the rose of sleep;
Across my lips I felt the night-breath, cold
 With spray of reefs, and heard the restless deep
Troubling the shore with movings manifold:
 I dropped the rose of sleep.

II.

Straightway mine eyes I raised: Before my bed
 One moved,—I saw the moonlight in her hair:
I.turned. The watcher's waxen torch was dead;
 He dreamed, forgetful, in his velvet chair.
" It was no wafture of the wind," I said;
 " The light was in her hair."

III.

Then I bethought me of the fever-fire
  That lately burned my life,—but I was calm;
I wearied not, nor wasted with desire
  Of mountain-snow or breath-reviving balm;
My heart beat lightly as a lover's lyre,
    · And all my veins were calm.

IV.

I looked beyond my window's trailing sprays
  (Stirred by that gust of passion from the sea):
I saw the grandeur of those heavenly ways
  That wait the ghostly journeyings of the FREE,
The forest-circling drifts of fallen haze,
    The gray and gusty sea.

V.

As one who need not haste, the moon on high
  Crossed the blue space from stellar sign to sign:
I saw her heedful acolytes supply

The feast of light: full softly she did shine.

From thoughts that hurt, the moon, that crossed

. the sky, .

Did sign me with a sign.

VI.

" On such a night," I mused, " for angels meet,

O Love long-lost! we heard the trampling deep;

And what we said the angels will repeat,

When in their snowy arms we lie asleep:

Not Death shall drown us from their voices sweet,

Albeit his floods are deep.

VII.

" We trod the surf-washed promontory, pale

As that wan foam beneath us: we must part.

Not less we laughed—the grief to countervail;

Sang our light songs, and found the honeyed

heart

Of many a blossomed rhyme; though every gale

Went whispering—we must part.

VIII.

" We talked of desert-people; how they make
    The dewless ways their place, the palm their tent,
And watch the red sand-whirlwinds overtake
    And wrap their loaded camels, travel-spent.
' That were a life not ill,' we gaily spake:
        ' The desert-palm our tent.'

IX.

" We told of wives who dare the torrid glade,
    Nor quake to hear at hand the lion roar;
Of queens who walk the scaffold undismayed,
    Whereon their loved have met the axe before.
' It were not hard to do,' we softly said;
        ' Love heeds no lion's roar.'

X.

" At this we turned,—and lo, that plant of Love
    (The fragrant snow of snows), was all in flower!
Its opening sweetness while we leaned to prove,
    Our first long kiss sublimed the regnant hour.

What more we said the seraphs sang above;
    Love's plant was all in flower.

XI.

" Ah, that last night! ' Peace crown thee, Sweet,'
    I said:
' Behold, her moonbeams linger in thine hair!'
She answered low: ' When past is all we dread,
    And Heaven for thee lets down its bridges fair,
Thy friend will wait before thy silent bed,
    The moonlight in her hair.' "

XII.

" Will wait." . . . . I raised mine eyes: the
    heavens were white;
Against his reefs I saw the sea prevail;
And borne abroad, those wreathing mists of night,
    Torn in the wanton wanderings of the gale;
Within my room that sanctitude of light:
    I felt my soul prevail.

XIII.

"And art thou here?" I cried; "and hast thou
  crossed,
  For me, the airy boundaries of the sky;
With summer-spicèd fruits and wines of cost,
  The sweetness of thy love to verify;
To kiss the lips of Death and melt his frost
    With breathings of the sky?"

XIV.

Thereat, with haste, a gathering darkness came,
  In which the sea and sky were wrapped away,
With star and moony disk: save one fair flame
  That on its silver plumage made delay.
Ere yet my soul its further thought could frame,
  The world was whelmed away,—

XV.

Save one pure flame: I saw its gleamy light,
  Pale as the shadeless vesture of the dead,

Pause and beat back the filming waves of night,

    Thou lost, my Love! from round thy drooping
        head.

O mine! my friend! swayed from seraphic flight:

    And I had called thee DEAD!

XVI.

What subtle, stealthy tides essayed to rise,

    That all my soul should bathe in healing dews?

Beneath the tender watching of thine eyes,

    The smiling of thy lips, I could not choose

But lapse into the rest that satisfies

    The soul with balmy dews.

XVII.

O sloth supreme! O silent floods and cold!

    From far-off shores, across the moonless deeps,

There came a grieving voice that cried: " Behold,

    How all is lost!   Our friend forever sleeps! "

And I arose,—as if a wind had rolled

    And cleft the moonless deeps.

XVIII.

Then as a new-wrought star, whose clouds are
gone,
Caught in a solar snare,—all unafraid
I moved; and lo, the zones, aflame with dawn,
Were populous with ghosts in snow arrayed!
I heard thy singing voice, and, Heavenward
drawn,
I answered, unafraid.

XIX.

O, blithe the fire-nerved frame and swift the flight!
Sweet, fold thine arms about me: grief is done.
Yet lest thy smile be somewhat vailed from sight,
Turn thou thy face an instant from the sun.
Ah, quivering kiss! . . . . Nay, Love engenders
light:
Behold, the night is done!

MOTHER.

I.

"Since near me cureless invalids bide
  Who pine in darkened rooms," I said,
    "Where bitterly that hour they wait
When they from mortal sight shall glide,
  Discarnate (never name them dead),
    I, sorrowing long, who sank of late
Even to the lips in silent seas,
To comfort me will comfort these.

II.

"Too well I know they get no ease,
  But suffer, suffer night and day;
    They never fill the weary lungs
· Beneath yon lichen-crusted trees

With soft and odorous airs of May;
 Nor seek her golden adder-tongues,
The flowers her pencilling hand adorns,
Her crinkle-roots and squirrel-corns.

III.

" Health-rosy as the rosy morns,
 They follow not the pebbled streams
  That down the hollows drip and dash;
Nor hasten home, when twilight warns,
 To tranquil rest and balmy dreams;
  Nor rise full early, lift the sash,
Lean out, let sunrise startle sight
With furnace-colors, blinding-bright.

IV.

" Now shall it be my one delight
 To cull and cluster bloom and leaf—
  Their dewy growth my daily task;
And if the breathing beauties slight

But for a moment banish grief
    From these poor hearts, no more I ask:
Dear were the sick, and very dear,
To her who fell asleep last year.

V.

" And should her spirit hover near,
    As some would say and as I think
      (For she was never far and slow,
If any neighbor wanted cheer,
    But smoothed the pillow, poured the drink,
      And made her deeds her kindness show),—
She will be glad my flowers to see,
Solace the sad and solace me.

VI.

"And though her garden fairer be
    (Why disbelieve she breaks the soil
      To drop those Heaven-perfected seeds?)
Coming and going, holy-free,

She may observe my loving toil;

  May smile approval, know my needs,

And, all unseen, my heart-strings thrill

With mother-praises, spirit-still."

VII.

So back and forth, with eager will,

  I trod my small inclosure round,

    Through every leisure, able hour,

To shape the circle, sow the drill,

  Make fine the pulverable ground,

    And fondly dream of bud and flower.

"Grow! grow!" I cried: "awake and stir!

If only for the love of her."

VIII.

Did any embryo defer

  To lift the plumule, faintly green,

    I did not spare to fume and fret,

And all impatiently aver

The nights were cold, the land was lean,
 The surface baked, the subsoil wet;
Until, in spite of tremulous doubt,
The latest sort began to sprout.

IX.

Then in, across, and round about,
 By angle, parallel and curve,
  With much transplanting, careful-slow,
I wrought my pleasant fancies out,
 Panting and ill and weak of nerve.
  "And this," I mused, "she used to grow
For perfume; this for grace of form;
And this for color deep and warm.

X.

"And this for blackness,—never storm
 Wore inkier hues; this lemon-bell
  For never-withering fragrant green;
And this, that butterflies might swarm

To sip its delicate hydromel;
   And this for modesty of mien
And whiteness: this for rarest hue,—
She loved to call it 'Heavenly blue.' "

XI.

Right thriftily the seedlings grew:
   And I went searching, day by day,
     For axil-shoot and clasping scale,
Whence buds might issue, fair and new:
   Till tempering clouds were burned away,
     And all the sky was Summer pale
Before the time; the weeks passed by,
Dew ceased to fall and wells were dry.

XII.

Another noon my plants must die.
   Half-blind with looking for the mist
     Through sunset-fires that scorched the
       brain,
9

I sought my couch with many a sigh,
  Faithless as any atheist:
    "It will not, will not, will not rain!"
I sobbed; but weeping, dropped asleep,
Or sank in trancèd silence deep.

XIII.

I say not Love the dream may keep
  As verity; nor, idly fond,
    Would sacred truth with falsehood leaven:
But sleepers walk where athletes creep;
  And what may break the during bond
    That brings the mother out of Heaven,
To prove and evermore make good
The tenderness of motherhood?

XIV.

And lo, within my sight she stood!
  She gravely gazed, she dimly smiled;
    Had well rebuked,—but all her heart,

As never heart of mortal could,
    Within her melting for her child,
        Seemed welling up to take my part,
Excuse the fault, the merit claim:
She might not praise, she would not blame.

XV.

But nearer, nearer while she came,
    She brought, upon her open palms,
        An earth-bound root, that angel-lore
Had surely named some hallowed name
    Beneath inviolable calms,—
        So white the single flower it bore.
And "Set the plant," she uttered low,
"Among your other plants to grow."

XVI.

I took the glistening green and snow:
    "Mother, I thank you," then I said;
        "I never saw a bloom so pure:

But tell me if the name you know."

   Her eyes in mine their sweetness shed;

     Soft was her voice as bells that lure

From far the wandering soul to prayer:

"The flower of Patience: give it care."

XVII.

Between us swam the dizzying air,—

   I reached my arms, I lost the sight;

     Within my ear the music failed.

First darkness; then a scarlet glare;

   Burst the long thunder through the night,

     Peal hurled on peal; the wild winds wailed;

As though some Heavenly sea to drain,

Came down the rain! came down the rain!

ONE OF THE TWELVE.

[After death, in converse with his brethren.]

I.

THEY answered, "What is that to us?
See thou to that. . . . Who bids the dead to rise
Himself shall die.   Is he not blasphemous? ·
Full of sedition—prophesying lies?
It shall be seen if he be marvellous!"

II.

Woe unto me for mine offense!
These thirsted, as the lions when they spring,
And in the bended neck of Innocence
Fasten their whited teeth and pant and cling:—
Be sure till they have drunk they go not thence.

III.

I flung them down their thirty coins—
The silver Cæsars shedding blood as rain;
I fled, as lepers flee, whom no man joins,—
Who shriek, through covered lips, from camp to
plain,
Struck deep with scall—accursed in life and
loins.

IV.

Lo, yet, if him they chanced to meet,
Their burning flesh, as foam of Galilee,
Grew cool and soft,—through spikenard danced
their feet:
But I—the earth me hated and the sea!
Him had I sold who made the lepers sweet.

V.

Him had I stricken dumb, who sealed
The mouths of rending spirits. Fair was he,—

Most lowly fair, as lilies of the field:
He made the lame to walk, the blind to see;
  Him, if one touched, that hour his hurt was
    healed.

VI.

  Weeping, he comfort gave who drew
From out the Heaven of heavens that flying dove:
  Him wonderful, the holy prophets knew,—
Who from the tender branches of his love
  Fed, as with grapes, the Gentile and the Jew.

VII.

  Them if he taught, "*Blessed are they—*
The poor, the merciful—they shall rejoice,"
  Like singing birds the laden went their way:
Now had the tuneful harpings of his voice
  Become as thunders of the LORD, that slay.

VIII.

  My feet, which late he washed, the sward

Disdained to bear; my flesh, his wine had cheered,
  Self-hung, fell down, spurned of the knotted
    cord:
No vengeful sword my bursting eyeballs seared,—
  My SIN, the sword, against my life, that
    warred.

IX.

A spirit clothed upon with flame,
(As when that multitude the lanterns brought
And over Cedron's brook with weapons came,
That I should hail and kiss him whom they
    sought,)
I, Judas, issuing, put the night to shame.

X.

None valiant stood my course to stay,
Slinging the stone that I should fall thereby;
  None terrible, whom evil ones obey:
Not Cain nor Lamech, driven of Him, MOST HIGH,
  Nor winged Abaddon, raging for his prey.

XI.

If any sun, across the vault,
To Hermon's cliffs me traitorous might aid,
  That I, upon their topmost snows should halt,
I scarched as those of Sodom, all afraid,
  Nor quenched me in their wretched sea of salt.

XII.

That emptiness wherein I trode
Was spread with odors foul,—as it had kept
  The four days dead, who there corruption
    strowed,   •
Till one had stood without, had groaning wept,
  Had cried *"Come forth ! "*—with whom the life
    abode.

XIII.

Down-reaped and garnered as the grain,
How went that sleeper out, loosed hand and foot!
  Me might he so have loved, me called amain;

For this the curse was on me branch and root:

 Who raised the dead, him had I kissed and
   slain.

XIV.

 If but the outermost to find,
Of that black-hollowed sepulchre, full wide,
 I journeyed on, far-going as the wind . . . .
How sweet his voice upon the mountain-side!
 "*Thee have I chosen:*"—Wherefore was he
   kind?

XV.

 Did he not know if once the springs
Ran out red blood, that I should dip and drink?
 Was he not lifted, as on eagles' wings?
If he but spake, did not the tempest sink?
 Who slayeth not the adder, ere he stings?

XVI.

 How with a whirlwind swept and piled,

The money-changers fled—blown out as leaves!
 "*The place of prayer*," he said, "*ye have
    defiled;*
My FATHER's *house ye make a den of thieves.*"
Did I not rob the poor?—On me he smiled.

XVII.

Fiercely within me wrought my deed;
Without, the midnight was as it were not:
My heart did sow abroad its fiery seed,—
Yea, heated as a furnace seven times hot,
  Itself upon itself did turn and feed.

XVIII.

Dread as a cloud whose lightning threats,
Now came I to a sea, walled East and West,—
  Even that whereby they toiled, who cast their
    nets
When from their ship the hungered souls be blest,
  Who drew them, great with what the surge
    begets.

XIX.

Scattered were they who him obeyed:
"*Abide in me,*" he spake; "*I am the vine.*"
How were they desolate and all dismayed!
Or ever of his fruit the boughs gave sign,
    Iscariot, at the root, the axe had laid.

XX.

O cities nine!   O region swept
With plagues, where late he dwelt!   On all that
    coast,
None lifted up the head, none wailed or wept.
There did the violent floods make stormy boast,
    And none their rage rebuked. . . .   The Mas-
    ter slept.

XXI.

Neared I such desert-land as girds
The templed mountain and the palmy groves,—
    Strown round with multitudes, like famished
    herds

Which none had watched: For such he brake
    the loaves,
The while they loved him for his peaceful
    words.

XXII.

Twelve did he choose: "*Go forth,*" he
    said;
"*Be even as I, the fallen ones to lift:*
Cast ye the devils out, raise up the dead." . . .
What had I rendered him for this, his gift?
Had I not killed my Lord, these had been fed.

XXIII.

Palsied and leprous, maimed and sick—
How had they leaped and laughed, new-cleansed
    and clothed!
Haply myself had made these dead men quick
(ONE working in me) . . . . Them to see I loathed:
About that place the pestilence was thick.

XXIV.

Upon me were His terrors turned:
As Eden's cherubim had fenced the sod
  With wings that high as Abel's offering burned,
As I had heard the awful Voice of GOD,
  Helped on of mighty winds the rocks I spurned.

XXV.

Albeit His wrath JEHOVAH curbs,
Behold His glittering sword he stays to whet!
  Beneath my fleeing feet, that crushed the herbs,
Forth sprang the blood,—my raiment all was wet:
  I sped as one whose heel the grave disturbs.

XXVI.

Forthwith the buried ones uprose;
They sorely pressed—they smote me while they
      spake:
  " Shall earth, before her season, feel the throes?

The seals wherewith He sealed us dost thou
    break?
Wilt thou, withal, our nakedness disclose?

XXVII.

"How had we lain and slept?" they cried,
" Bound with the scented linen fine and clean;
    Till, as a bridegroom seeking for his bride,
Our Lord had come, and, with his arrows keen,
    Had slain that king with whom the dead abide!

XXVIII.

"How had we risen, arrayed as flowers!
Whiter than fuller's cloth had we been white—
    So had he made his noontide splendor ours;
That we should feast among the sons of light,
    How had he led us through the olive-bowers!"

XXIX.

Bitter that I his life had spilt,

As waves of thronging seas they round me surged.
  Meantime if any refuge had been built
For such as I, whom these avengers urged,
  I sought to enter in and hide my guilt.

XXX.

  When lo, the city! she who scorns
Her King; who wastes the costly ointment sweet;
  Nor yet for wedding-mirth her house adorns;
Now did I think to reach the mercy-seat,
  And lay mine hands upon the altar-horns.

XXXI.

  Scourged thither, whence of late I fled,
Deep sick was I, as one his wound who probes:
  That I, where him I wronged, might vail my
        head,
Might rend from off my limbs their filthy robes,
  Great were my wrestlings with the fleshless
        dead.

XXXII.

Ere yet the scarlet courts I neared,
The mountains trembled and the crags were torn;
Him I beheld upon the cross upreared;
Whom I betrayed, forsaken there did mourn.
He on Elohim called. . . . . Now first I feared!

XXXIII.

Him did the prince of Hell assault—
That serpent whom the sons of men accuse;
Yea, Death his crest did verily exalt,
That he, the well-belovéd son should bruise—
One altogether lovely, without fault,

XXXIV.

Meekly the Christ gave up the ghost . . . .
New saw I him in glistening beauty clad,
Brighter than he who leads the starry host,
White-walking with the dead—them making glad;
Among their shining throngs he shining most.

XXXV.

As one the crimson bolt who shuns
With lifted hands, down at his feet I fell:
  More naked than the gnawed and dreadful
      ones,—
Self-stripped and shamed. . . . On me his eyes did
      dwell,
  As they, for light, had gathered up the suns.

XXXVI.

Now was I smitten with the sword:
Even pierced to the dividing of the joints,—
  Cut down and withered like the prophet's gourd.
As one for burial who his child anoints,
  On me the vials of his love he poured.

XXXVII.

For me, of murderers most abhorred,
With Death he darkly strove; behold, he wept!
  "Eli," he cried, " *me, sorrowful, reward!* ". . .

As I, full sweet, beneath the flowers had slept,
All fair as they, I rose—and kissed my Lord.

XXXVIII.

Lo, meet for salts of Judgment, shorn
And all despoiled—among the twelve the least
Among the poor and vile, that one forlorn,—
Yet was I bidden to the marriage-feast:
Honey, with honeycomb, and oil, and corn.

SONNETS.

" If a man die shall he live again ? "

149

·I.

ALL pleasant are the greenwoods where abide
  Soft-hued Hepaticas and wind-flowers pale,
The shaly clefts where streaked herb-Roberts hide,
  The slants where droop the harebells fairy-frail;
And pleasant are the marshes mallow-rosed,
  The grassy dips that hold the shallow ponds,
The waterfalls through flood-torn banks disclosed,
· The haunts where ferns uncurl their delicate
      fronds;
And pleasant are the glooms of towering pines,
  Moss-beds whose scarlet-dotted tufts secrete
Low wintergreens white-globed, and partridge-
      vines,
  Twin-leaved, twin-tubed, faint-tinged and per-
      fect sweet;
Full pleasant are the pink-boughed laurel-bowers
Where children climb and cling and load their
      hands with flowers.

II.

Up, mourning soul! Why for the Dead remain
    In Grief's illimitable caverns mute?
    Herein shall hills their leaping pulses drain,
    Nor yield thee any profit, bloom or fruit;
Her sombre doors against thy feet made fast,
    Still must thou, groping, track this aislèd snare,
Deep in some ghastly grave-room plunge at last,
    Touch crumbling hands?   (Oh, once their brows
            were fair
Who now from Summer gladness lie aloof!)
    Call thou, and cry: if any tempest lower,
Bid thou its bolts thy sealèd jail unroof;
    Or if, far down, the terrible Earthquake cower,
With tremblings as of one whom fears prevent,
Command thou that these rock-wrought fastnesses
            be rent.

III.

My little torch, uplifted, lights me round
  The drear earth-chambers: Here a stony rose,
And there a goblet dashed upon the ground:
  But never dew exhales, or sweet wine flows
From mimic flask or tankard; never drips
  Down bowls ancestral Love's metheglin clear—
Bee-plunderings, fitly strained for poet-lips.
  Beneath immeasurable vaults I veer
The kindled brand, nor gild unfeatured night
  Beyond an arm-reach; now some water-ink,
To light impervious, blanks the downward sight,
  And stays the search; and now, in truth, I think
To shriek so loud the very dead must rise,
Break through immuring walls, let sun into mine
      eyes.

IV.

THE Dead. . . Ah, verily not asleep they lie!
　So bitter-loved they are, they needs must live.
And hear—though Hades smother up the cry,
　And every volant zephyr prove a sieve
To spill the sounds.　What then remains to do
　But call and call?　Be certain they will come,
Dispart the rocks, to outward climbings woo;
　Voicing their proud "We are!" strike Sorrow
　　　　　dumb;
Harping "We shall be!" thrill the resonant deeps
　With roar of echoes—shake reverberant earth,
Smite down, demolish intercluding steeps,
　Exalt and fill with everlasting mirth
Their dear-beloved—no more to dwell and dwine
In hollows subterrene, dark-locked from things
　　　　divine.

V.

AND healthful are the tamarack-scented airs,

    Deep vale-suspirings, upland-breathings keen,

Out-blowings of the mountain-gale that shares

    That smell of rifts where berried cedars lean;

Healthful the swift surf-ploughing trade-winds all,

    Sky-coursing blasts that roll the thunder-wains,

Far-whirled cyclones that make the forests fall,

    Black, unresisted, levelling hurricanes;

And healthful are the shinings of the noon,

    Mist-emanations thin as spectral shroud,

Dew-gatherings, driftings dense that blot the
        moon,

    Rain-sprinklings cool, down-pourings of the
        cloud.

Stand forth, cave-prophet:—Wind and earth-
        quake-din,

Then fire: the still, small Voice, and lo, the LORD
        therein!

VI.

Soul, be thou humble: It is good to hear

The cooing of the babes, their gurgling speech,

Child-wonderings, when the sly gusts interfere,

And sail the rainbow-bubbles out of reach;

To hear the young laugh out where skaters throng,

The free sled-riders shout in coasting-time,

True-lovers murmur, mothers croon the song,

Choirs chant loud anthems when the church-
bells chime;

Better to hear the prayings of the old

Who wait Death's ocean-deep baptismal rite,

Who, sighing, sink in slow submergings cold,

Who soar, exulting, vailed from narrow sight.

Oh, best, on hushed and holy heights to meet,

And hear, from spirit-lips, familiar words and
sweet!

VII.

Soul, be thou pure: Rise, clean as river-flowers
  From out the soil and slime, the covered shame,
As sweet-bay blossom-cups that gather showers,
  Whose tree-upholden whiteness none can blame;
Pure as thrice-winnowed snow on peaks of Ind,
  .As North-fire flickerings up the starry ways,
As planet glancings, streamings of the wind
    That sweeps the splendors far when comets
        blaze;
As beamings of the central Sun that warms
  The uttermost concealments of the night,
Our one-revolving Universe informs
  With awful inter-penetrating light
Infused from Godhead; pure as are the blest
That on the Infinite Bosom smiling lean and rest.

VIII.

Soul, be thou not remote and slow to love:
   Be as the flakes that on the snowdrop melt,
Making the sweet more sweet; as fumes above
   Full incense-vases where the coals have dwelt,
Whose odoriferous atoms, smoking out
   From gum and stacte, onycha and myrrh,
Infold the righteous and the undevout;
   Be thou as Eden's atmosphere astir
With walkings of the Lord; be as the fire
   To snow-bewildered wanderers; as the sun
To dungeon-wretches—life's fulfilled desire;
   As altar-flame when sacrifice is done;
As burning furnace-heats, where unalarmed
Thy loved shall enter in, meet God, and move
     unharmed.

IX.

AND beautiful shall on the mountains be
    The feet of them that bring good tidings down,
That haste to publish peace ; and thou shalt see,
    Yet in thy flesh, thy MAKER: He shall crown
Thy days with ecstasies, thy nights with calms;
    And He shall make thee rich with meal and
        wine,
With fatness of the flocks, with powders, balms,
    With milk and honey, clusters of the vine,
Olives, pomegranates, dates and mandrakes
        sweet;
    And thou shalt bid the sick, the halt, the
        blind,
In to the feast; and thou shalt bathe their feet
    With smelling ointments; thou their wounds
        shalt bind,
Therein the precious oil of healing pour;
And thou shalt feed His poor, withholding not
        thy store.

X.

THE holy ones shall cover not from thee
  The brightness of their faces where they shine:
From that all-cold sepulture of the sea
  Thou   shalt   come forth;   and lo,   the Hand
        Divine
Shall so uplift thee, thou shalt surely hear
  The four-and-twenty elders say: "All things
Thou hast created, LORD!" and thou shalt near
  The golden altar where the incense clings—
Sweet, sweet, most sweet with prayers of all the
        saints!
Shalt see the golden censer, filled with fire,
Cast into earth, whence rose thy long complaints;
  Shalt hear the creatures four, whose great
        desire
Rests not, forever say (thyself not dumb):
  " Worthy the LORD, which WAS, and IS, and IS
        TO COME! "